Anonym

New Selves

Issues of Identity in the Caribbean Canadian Poetry of Claire Harris and Olive Senior

Bibliographic information published by the German National Library:

The German National Library lists this publication in the National Bibliography; detailed bibliographic data are available on the Internet at http://dnb.dnb.de .

Copyright © 2010 Diplomica Verlag GmbH
Print and binding: Books on Demand GmbH, Norderstedt Germany
ISBN: 9783961165537

http://www.diplom.de/

Anonym

New Selves

Issues of Identity in the Caribbean Canadian Poetry of Claire Harris and Olive Senior

Diplom.de

Table of Contents

1 Introduction

In recent years, Caribbean literature is experiencing a revival as the growth in the number of publications by Caribbean authors as well as the resulting rise in scholarly criticism indicate. A number of reasons can account for this development. One important reason is that Toronto, or more generally speaking Canada, came to replace London as the centre of Caribbean literature, as David Chariandy states. Since the rapid rise in immigration, especially from the Caribbean islands, to Canada brought about a significant demographic change, the government launched a campaign to promote minority writers. This resulted in a significant growth of Caribbean literature in Canada.

It is to say that despite the fact that a strong sense of Caribbean identity connects a large number of literary works, it is essential to also be aware of their disparities since each author's work is influenced by their unique position in culture.

The aim of the following paper is an analyses of selected poems of Claire Harris and Olive Senior in regard of the theme that connects the poetic work of these two women writers – identity. At first glance, it might come as quite a surprise to some readers that the literary artist Harris and Senior share a connection in their poetical exploration of themes. However after having a short glance, a commonalty between them will became apparent. Due to the subject the essay is informed by concepts of feminism, post-colonialism and cultural studies in order to depict the different ways in which identity is addressed in their work.

I will argue that the ideas of identity that surface in the poetry of the two writers Harris and Senior all share certain characteristics marking their cultural positions, with all the differences and more importantly all the similarities that occur in their voicing of Caribbean Canadian diaspora identities of women. However, since the prevalent theme of the Caribbean self would vastly exceed the limitations of this paper, several limitations had to be made. First of all, I will limit myself to the genre of poetry. Another limitation is that only the three mayor aspects of Caribbean Canadian cultural identity can be taken into account. The first of these is these is the influence of gender in the formation of cultural identity as depicted in their poetry. Next is the impact of colonial history on the post-colonial subject, and the last topic is the question of home and exile, or more generally speaking of belonging.

2 Why is identity an issue in Canadian Caribbean women poetry?

2.1 Perceptions of gender

One important factor in shaping individual identity is the concept of gender. As critics have repeatedly drawn attention to the fact that the surge in women poets has resulted in giving a new perspective to common themes in Caribbean poetry (Brown and McWatt XXXI), among them identity, it seems to be necessary to evaluate the impact of gender on identity in Harris's and Senior's poetry as well. For women, identity is even more important. (Gikandi 197ff) In her essay "Why Do I Write", Harris even explicitly stated that one of her main concerns in writing is to "[…] reveal what happens when a woman must deal with the realities of racial as well as gender subjugation" (Harris "Why Do I Write" 27). Among the several verses dealing with the role of gender in the formation of women's identity; Senior's "One Night, the Father" or "The Mother", Harris's "Nude On a Pale Staircase" or "Policemen Cleared in Jaywalking Case"; the paper will focus on the formation of gender roles in Caribbean society to evaluate their influence on individual identity. Therefore it will be attempted to first analyse "Birdshooting Season" by Olive Senior and subsequently "Child This Is the Gospel On Bakes" by Claire Harris in regard to the influences of gender.

In the following paragraph the poem "Birdshooting Season" is to be discussed in relation to gender, in order to explain how gender shapes the identity of Caribbean women. Senior's "Birdshooting Season" consists of four stanzas of irregular length; four, six, two and five lines respectively (Senior "Birdshooting Season"). The first stanza of "Birdshooting Season" seems to describe the gathering of men at the father's house of the speaker in the night before the bird shooting out of a children's perspective, while the second verse seems to describe the women's various activities of preparing provisions for the men (ll. 1-10). Further, the second stanza enables the reader to recognize the setting as Jamaica, because typical Jamaican food and drinks are mentioned: "[…] cerassie/ wrap pone and tie-leaf" (ll. 7-8). Critic Renate Papke also commented on Senior's use of alliteration "[…] men/ make marriages with their guns/ My father's house turns macho" (ll. 1-2) and "[…] contentless women/ stir their brews: hot coffee/ chocolate; cerassie" (ll. 5-8) to illustrate the concept of gender in Caribbean society (115). Even though it is obvious to the speaker of the poem that the women do not approve of the bird shooting, as they describe them as "[...] contentless women" (l. 5), they nonetheless do not voice their discontent regarding the hunt but rather support the men with their preparations. In addition Senior here points out the traditional gender roles in the Caribbean family, according to her remark in *Working Miracles: Women's Lives in the English-Speaking Caribbean* "[t]here seems to be [a] widespread acceptance of this practice among all classes, of females catering to males and of failing to make them assume responsibilities for domestic activities[...]" (Senior *Working Miracles: Women's Lives in the English-Speaking Caribbean* 35). The male participants of the hunt are free to spend the night drinking "[...] white rum neat" (ll. 10), whereas the women in the house prepare their provisions for the occasion. "Birdshooting Season" continues with a couplet depicting the men leaving the house very early in the morning to go on their hunt, followed by the last stanza of the poem. In the last stanza describes how the children watch the men leave. Also, it seems probable that the speaker of the poem is a little girl, as the speaker refers to the group of children:

> We stand quietly on the
> doorstep shivering. Little boys
> longing to grow up birdhunters too
> Little girls whispering:
> Fly Birds Fly (ll. 13-17)

Senior's often employs the child's point of view in her works, though mostly in her short-stories, to criticise adult society (Pollard 541). In this case it seems as if she makes use of this technique to question traditional gender roles. On the one hand the boys want to become hunters just like their fathers (Papke 115). On the other hand, the girls appear to have accepted that they are helpless in this patriarchal society, as they only dare to whisper their hopes that the birds might be able to escape their hunters. Much in the same way their mothers are unable to voice their contempt for the hunt. In contrast to Papke's interpretation of the women's reaction, as having lost empathy for the birds (115), I would rather argue that it is not acceptable for women in their culture to overtly criticize men (Boyce Davies 52). This would correlate with a statement Senior made in an interview with Anna Rutherford. Senior noted that she wants to dismantle the myth of the "black matriarch" as "[...] the myth disguises the fact of her powerlessness in the wider society" (Rutherford 98). Like Senior, Harris portrays the powerlessness of women through the perspective of a child in "Child This Is the Gospel on Bakes" ("Child   This Is the Gospel on Bakes").

"Child   This Is the Gospel on Bakes" is taken from *Drawing Down a Daughter*, when the female speaker of the poem talks about traditional family recipes and the women associated with them:

> Girl   all of us in this family know how to make float   how
> to make bakes   the real thing   and acra   not even
> your father's mother make so good   and pilau   and
> callaloo with crab & salt pork   barefoot rice   rich black
> cake   cassava pone   (is true your Carib great aunto on your
> dad side teach your mother that) but the coconut ice cream
> and five-fingers confetti   buljol   souse   those are our
> things (Harris *Drawing Down a Daughter* 44)

More important than all listed Trinidadian dishes, is the sense of family history and culture they convey though (Williams "Claire Harris and the Poetic Shape of Women's Words" 70). After her thoughts have pondered on the different recipes she knows and the female relatives from whom she learned them, she remembers an evening when she was making pastry with her mother in her childhood, which is where "Child   This Is the Gospel on Bakes" begins. In her description of the scene the social reinforcement of gender roles becomes apparent. Besides being taught her family's recipes, which could be seen as Harris implying the girl's introduction to female domesticity, it additionally represents women's confinement to the house or rather private sphere in Caribbean society. Moreover the speaker is also scolded for being a dreamer by someone stating "[...] 'this child always dreaming yes/ but what you going to do with her'" (Harris "Child   This Is the Gospel on Bakes" 163). Thus the young girl is discouraged from following her ambitions and is instead expected to live up to female gender roles. Yet her mother replies "[...] 'let her dream/ while she can' [...]" (Harris "Child   This Is the Gospel on Bakes" 163), as she is well aware of the fact that her daughter will only have little time left before she has to eventually give up her dreams. Dannabang Kuwabong reads the mother's reply as signifying her understanding of her daughter's dreams for a better life than hers (Kuwabong 134). Further, the speaker watches a boy playing outside "[...] a small boy barefeet/ on the plum tree his voice shrilling king/ of the mountain threats   old voice eggs him on" (Harris "Child   This Is the Gospel on Bakes" 162-63). In contrast to her being scolded for dreaming, the boy is encouraged by an old man in the yard to explore his environment. Only a few lines further in the poem, it becomes obvious that the young girl has already started to accept her role by stating "[...] the way girls should/ waiting patiently for evening" (Harris "Child   This Is the Gospel on Bakes" 163). As the child kneads the dough for the pastry, she reflects on "[...] the recurring dream in which she climbs/ through a forest of leaves[...]" (Harris "Child   This Is the Gospel on Bakes" 163-64) chasing after a bird. This dream could be interpreted as visualizing her desire for personal freedom in a patriarchal society that restricts her to the private sphere. Another aspect of her dreams is that it shows that even though the girl is consciously aware of her role in society, she nonetheless has an unconscious desire to break free of imposed gender conventions. Albeit being better in cricket, she does not recall receiving support in her pursuit of this activity, but moreover is judged by her female relatives and the kitchen maid solely on her ability to produce perfectly round bakes, meaning her housekeeping skills. "The art of baking a perfectly rounded cake (against all odds), is a metaphor for negotiating the intricacies of life dominated by patriarchy" (134), points out Kuwabong. For this reason her mother tries to help her adjust to society by showing her a trick to make round bakes (Harris "Child   This Is the Gospel on Bakes" 164). Yet, at the same time the mother is instructing her daughter on how to please her father's and society's gender expectations (Kuwabong 134), as she suggests to her daughter to "[…] decorate [hers] with a fork   dad will be proud" (Harris "Child   This Is the Gospel on Bakes" 164). It should be further noted that the adverb accentuating the mother's utterances could be argued to be informed by silence. Take, for example, "her mother saying ever so carefully [...]" (Harris "Child   This Is the Gospel on Bakes" 163) or "her mother says gently [...]" (Harris "Child   This Is the Gospel on Bakes" 164). Remarkably similar to the women in Senior's verse "Birdshooting Season", Harris portrays women in "Child   This Is the Gospel on Bakes" as unable to speak their mind. Comments by Carol Boyce Davies and Elaince Savory Fido about women's voicelessness could well apply to both writers verses:

> "The concept of voicelessness necessarily informs any discussion of Caribbean women and literature. [...] By voicelessness we also mean silence; the inability to express a position in the language of the 'master' as well as the textual construction of a woman as silent. Voicelessness also denotes articulation that goes unheard." (Boyce Davies 52)

Yet, they also note that women's voicelessness cannot merely be attributed to gender, but also results from colonialism. Therefore the paper will continue with an examination of the impact of colonialism on Caribbean identity.

2.2 History of Colonialism

The colonial past could be said to have left a mark on the sense of Caribbean people's identity, as its aftermath continues to influence their self-image as well as their perception by others. To get our discussion on a concrete footing, let us consider some examples dealing with the influence of the colonial past on cultural as well as individual identity in verses by Senior and Harris. "Meditation on Yellow", "The Lady" as well as "Cockpit Country Dreams" by Senior and Harris's "Nude On A Pale Staircase" or her prose-poem *Drawing Down A Daughter* would be cases in point. Unfortunately, space prevents us from examining the aforementioned verses in detail. The paper will however proceed with an analysis of two different poems, beginning with a discussion of Claire Harris's "Policeman Cleared In Jaywalking Case". Afterwards, a well-known poem by Olive Senior, "Colonial Girls School", receives detailed treatment. It will become apparent, that while both works of poetry deal with the legacy of colonialism, they also differ in some aspects.

In "Policeman Cleared in Jaywalking Case", Harris artistically reflects on an actual case of jaywalking that occurred in Canada. Scholar Emily Allen Williams refers to this technique as 'biographical in[ter]vention' (Williams "Triadric Revelations of Excilic Identity: Claire Harris's *Fables from the Women's Quarters, Dipped in Shadow*, and *She*" 182). Harris's poem begins with an excerpt from an article in the Edmonton Journal reporting that "the city policeman who arrested a/ juvenile girl for jaywalking [...]/ has been cleared of any wrongdoing by/ the Alberta law enforcement appeal/board" (Harris "Policeman Cleared in Jaywalking Case" 48). Without any further explanation, the article lists the procedures and examinations the girl had to endure, resulting in her being jailed in an adult detention centre (Harris "Policeman Cleared in Jaywalking Case" 48). What is even more striking for the reader is that the reason given for the policeman's action is that "[...] the girl/ had not co-operated during the first five/ minutes after she was stopped [...]" (Harris "Policeman Cleared in Jaywalking Case" 48). After the supposedly impartial description in the newspaper article, Harris gives a short definition of the verb 'to signify'. This term could be seen as correlating to the central subject of Harris's "Policeman Cleared in Jaywalking Case" (Williams "Claire Harris and the Poetic Shape of Women's Words" 55), since it "[...] indicates an act of acknowledgement of sharing, of identifying with" ("Policeman Cleared in Jaywalking Case" 182). Owing to an incident of jaywalking in her youth greatly resembling the fifteen year old girl's experience, the black female speaker feels compelled to lend voice to the experiences of discrimination and abuse for those who, as Williams but it are ignored by society (Williams "Triadric Revelations of Exilic Identity: Claire Harris's *Fables from the Women's Quarters, Dipped in Shadows*, and *She*" 182). Next, Harris gives the reader more information on this case of jaywalking. Accordingly, the reader is forced to revaluate their assessment of the newspaper extract, because it says that the young girl handed her bus pass to the officer as means of identification. In addition a possible reason for her not co-operative behaviour is given, for "[a]n eyewitness to the street incident described her/ as 'terrified'" (Harris "Policeman Cleared in Jaywalking Case" 49). In is in this atmosphere of uncertainty on side of the reader that the actual poem starts.

The lyrical self of the poem begins as well as ends her part with the words "[l]ook you, child, I signify", though the refrain at the end slightly varies "[l]ook you child, I signify" (Harris "Policeman Cleared in Jaywalking Case" 49-50). Therefore the claim made in the preceding paragraph about the central importance of 'signifying' is underlined by the phrases' framing of the speaker's account. Harris uses the literary device of repetition several times in "Policeman Cleared in Jaywalking Case", although she repeatedly alternates her original phrases. One striking example for this observed technique is "[...] to stand to stand and say to stand and say be-/ fore you all   the child was black and female and therefore mine [...]" (Harris "Policeman Cleared in Jaywalking Case" 49). Here, the speaker adds something to the core of the phrase every time it is repeated, so that it reflects the speaker's struggle to build up enough courage to speak about her incident with jaywalking. The reason for her hesitation to speak about this incident are that she still feels apprehensive after all these years, since she was "[...] stripped/ down to skin and sex [...]" (Harris "Policeman Cleared in Jaywalking Case" 49). Consequently she identifies with the fifteen year old girl in the article, as she still remembers the effect racial and sexual discrimination had on her. Another literary device encountered in the poem is the metaphor of the edge.

"[Y]ou walk the edge of this cliff with me at your peril/ do not hope to set/ off safely to brush stray words off your face [...] and go home comfortably" (Harris "Policeman Cleared in Jaywalking Case" 49). Such are the words the speaker of the poem uses to convey her warning about the impact her story will have on the reader. According to her it is impossible to stay unaffected by the report she is about to give, because it exposes their society's racism. To communicate this message, Harris makes uses the metaphor of the edge. The edge stands for the black women's marginalization in Canadian society, which can no longer be ignored after bearing witness to her act of signifying. Similarly to the speaker of the poem, the female black reader will no longer feel secure in the white male society as its dangers are portrayed. Harris emphasises this message in several ways, by the numerous repetition of "white" (Harris "Policeman Cleared in Jaywalking Case" 49), which culminates in "[...] and here I stand black and female/ bright black on the edge of this white world [...]" (Harris "Policeman Cleared in Jaywalking Case" 49). Yet, in the face of sexual and racial discrimination Harris's speaker refuses to assimilate into racist society neither does she intend to "[...] fade into the midget shades" ("Policeman Cleared in Jaywalking Case" 49). Instead she identifies herself as "bright black [...]" (Harris "Policeman Cleared in Jaywalking Case"

49). However, she nonetheless indicates the problematic nature of her decision to retain her ethnic identity.

On the following page the reader receives more information on her dilemma by reiteration of fear. While Harris uses repetition yet again in "Policeman Cleared in Jaywalking Case" to reveal the narrator's fear of "[...] skeletal skin the spider/ tracery of your veins [...]" ("Claire Harris and the Poetic Shape of Women's Words" 50), or rather white society, it also serves to express the woman's fear of acculturation. It is an impression derived from the narrator's repetition of "[...] I fear myself [...] but I fear most myself how easy to/ drown in your world [...]" (Williams "Claire Harris and the Poetic Shape of Women's Words" 50). Williams expands on this view by commenting that "[...] the narrator speaks of how easy it is for blacks to become consumed by the white power structure" ("Claire Harris and the Poetic Shape of Women's Words" 56). The poem ends on a wary note on the menace of acculturation to white culture and the danger it represent for a Caribbean individual as well as cultural identity.

A vital tool in the indoctrination of culture is education, thus we will now turn an analytic eye on Senior's verse with this issue as central theme. In contrast to Harris, who focuses on the impact of colonialism on the legal system, Senior illuminates its influence on education. Yet, the central theme in both is the impact of the colonial past on the present-day lives of Caribbean people, be it in their native country or in exile. At the beginning of "Colonial Girls School", the narrator elucidates the outcome of her schooling at a colonial girls' school. The "[b]orrowed images" (l. 1) mentioned in the first stanza, caused the girls to feel inferior in comparison to the images instilled by their colonial education. This effect is achieved in several instances. First of all, perceptions of beauty are modelled on European ideals. To achieve these colonial ideals centring on whiteness/Europeanism, any traces of their black ancestry had to be erased consequently. Therefore not only did they try to make their skin seem pale (l. 2), but also their caretakers "dekinked our [their] hair" (l. 6). However, Senior here also ironically indicates that they could solely will their skins to be pale. Thus she critically comments on the fact that the taught model of beauty did not come naturally to the girls at the school, but was imposed on them by their colonial education. Secondly, the instructors are set to make the girls adopt European manners, which demands women to be quiet. Hence, their laughter and perceived loudness (l. 3-4) are silenced. The colonial culture which the girls are taught to adapt to, renders them as inferior due to their race and sex. As the girls are not able to achieve these standards, they are left with a feeling of their own inferiority. Thirdly, as Williams observes, "[...] they had little to no continuity to their arts and cultural practices and beliefs" (Williams "The Ancestral Quilt of Arawak, African, and European Influence in the Poetry of Olive Senior" 91).

As a result of the total erasure of their culture in their education, the girls perceive themselves as being worth nothing, indeed they seem to not exist at all. This impression is gained by the repetition of the word "nothing" in the couplets (ll. 12-13; 18-19; 24-25; 33-34; 40-41), which intersect the larger stanzas. Throughout the poem, two line stanzas are used to express the complete erase of their indigenous culture, which leads to the girls' feeling of being lost. Further, the curriculum consists of studying European literature (l. 16), as well as Latin (l. 15) and history (ll. 20-23). "She [Senior] highlights the *skill* of colonial historiographers in their selection of subjects and sources which render African geographical and ancestral placement as nonexistent [...]", stresses Williams in regard to Senior's examples of history topics, which exclude Jamaican, Caribbean or African history intentionally. Instead their education focuses on the history of places far from their own, prompting the students to react to their missing representation with once again feeling non-existent:

> Studying: *History Ancient and Modern*
> Kings and Queens of England
> Steppes of Russia
> Wheatfields of Canada
>
> There was nothing of our landscape there
> Nothing about us at all (ll. 20-25)

The speaker of the poem then proceeds to express her disregard for historical figures and events concerning racial conflicts, but instead emphasises that they have read Nicholas Vachel Lindsay's portrayal of blacks. Williams asserts that Senior contrasts political icons, Marcus Garvey and Lumumba, as well as an event of racial disturbances (Williams "The Ancestral Quilt of Arawak, African, and European Influence in the Poetry of Olive Senior" 92). Yet, the speaker nullifies their achievements by regarding Vachel Lindsay as more important, which is visualized by setting 'we' in italics (l. 31). This however is problematic, since it could mean that they have internalized his, according to Ickstadt's claim stereotypical and racist portrayal of black people in "Congo: A Study of the Negro Race" (Ickstadt 153). Senior alludes to the title of this specific poem in several ways. For one thing, the speaker references Lindsay with "[t]o us: mumbo-jumbo" (l. 30), and for another, she remarks that they have read his "vision of the jungle" (l. 32). Both remarks could be intertextual references to "Congo: A Study of the

Negro Race", as a line of Lindsay's verse goes: "Mumbo-Jumbo is dead in the jungle" (Lindsay 7).

Moving now to the aspect of language in the ninth stanza, Senior critically comments on the crucial position language has in ensuring cultural domination over others. The root cause is the devalorisation of their language, as stated in the remark by the speaker: "(For our language/ - 'bad talking'- detentions)" (ll. 37-39). It should be noted that the narrator of the poem parenthesises her statement, as if she does not venture to speak it out loud. Since the use of Jamaican Creoles poses a punishable offence, students are strongly discouraged to use it. In its place they are taught "Latin declensions" (l. 36). The consequence of being directed to strive for an unachievable integration into a colonial culture, while at the same being discouraged to retain their Jamaican culture, ultimately leads to a sense of alienation from both cultures. In spite of their indoctrination with European culture at the colonial girls school, the speaker now refuses to be controlled by "[...] those pale northern eyes [...]" (l. 12). Senior utilizes the stylistic device of repetition to describe the power of the "pale northern eyes" (ll. 12; 48-50), or rather European culture, over the speaker representing collective Jamaican society. At the end of the verse, the lyrical self asks a rhetorical question on how the European culture pales in comparison to the brighter future ahead of them at the present:

> For isn't it strange how
> northern eyes
> in the brighter world before us now
>
> Pale? (ll. 47-50)

Senior here plays on the different uses of the word 'pale', as she first uses it as an adjective in the poem and in the end as a verb. Her transformation of the 'pale' is illustrated by the separation of the word in the last line as well as by its capitalisation. Through having overcome the colonial doctrines, they are able to appreciate their indigenous culture more and are facing more promising days.

This change is described by Senior via the image of the broken mirror (l. 44). "The 'breaking' of the mirror is tantamount to the dismantling of the mirror-image of the Europeans which was trust upon African Jamaicans" ("The Ancestral Quilt of Arawak, African, and European Influence in the Poetry of Olive Senior" 93). With these words Williams delineates the speaker's reclamation of a distinct Jamaican cultural identity by discarding their forced appreciation of European ideals. The revocation of their forced acculturation is further symbolised by Senior's evocation of Anansi, "[...] the Akan trickster/spider-hero [...]" (Williams "The Ancestral Quilt of Arawak, African, and European Influence in the Poetry of Olive Senior" 93). It could be claimed that Anansi, as a major figure of originating from African culture, personifies/ stands for the indigenous Jamaican African culture. Therefore by letting him out of his bag (l. 46), they have liberated themselves from the colonial culture that was forced upon them and instead reclaimed their native culture. Overall "Colonial Girls School" is concerned with what Williams declares as important subject in Senior's verse, "[...] her concern with the mental bondage (which has continued beyond the physical bondage) of the African Jamaicans [...]" ("The Ancestral Quilt of Arawak, African, and European Influence in the Poetry of Olive Senior" 93). In this case the poem ends on a positive note tough, as the speaker is able to overcome the colonial erasure of her cultural identity and thus recover her sense of self.

2.3 Exile

"What still seems to be consistent, even in the face of continuous change, is the fact that the concept of home appears to be tied in some way with the notion of identity – the *story* we tell ourselves, which is also the story *others* tell of us" (Boi 175). This assertion was made by Paola Boi in regard to the importance of the concepts of home in Caribbean literature and culture in her essay "Homecomings without Home: Reconquering the Creole Identity through the Conquest of Discursive Space". The relevance of home in Caribbean society stems from the fact that home takes on a greater significance for those that leave their home country. As Stewart Brown and Mark McWatt conclude, "[...] 'exile' from the Caribbean had been an important feature of the literature and its creations and publication from the very beginning" (XXVIII). Exile is an experience that both, Senior and Harris share and as a result shapes their works, though Senior herself refuses the use of the term 'exile' to describe her condition. In an interview with Amatoritsero Ede called "Exile is Not My Name", Senior claims that she find the term unsuited as she lives in Toronto by choice and moreover is " free to go back to my homeland Jamaica- which I [she] do quite frequently" (Ede). However, migration to Canada did nonetheless shape her work, as it changed her perception of herself (Ede). Therefore, a discussion of her verse in relation to notions of home and exile is needed to clarify their influence on identity. As space in this paper does not allow to evaluation of her extensive body of works, "Leaving Home" has been selected as fine example. Towards the end of this chapter, issues of exilic identity will be determined in Harris's "Towards the Colour of Summer".

"Leaving Home" can be divided into two main parts with the first half of the poem describing the event of leaving home (ll. 1-14), while the second segment deals with homesickness (ll. 15-26). Last but not least, the last section of the poem further seems to offer a possible solution to the in-between state of a migrant identity. This thematic division of the poem seems rather warrantable, since the two halves begin with "one day[...]" (l. 1) and "[t]ill the day" (l. 15) respectively. Therefore a contrast between the conditions in the first and second half is presumably the case. First of all, Senior depicts a scene of departure from the subject's home. In contrast to her poems we have discussed so far, she here does not write out of the speaker's point of view but employs second person narration. Senior frequently employs parentheses in "Leaving Home", as if to comment on aspects that the subject feels insecure about or that are not talked about. This resembles Senior's use of parentheses in the previously discussed "Colonial Girls School". By way of illustration, consider the first instance of the parenthesised sentence. "[O]ne day, strength (from where, you don't know) to aim/ for the opening, to say: I am leaving" (ll. 1-3), where the parenthesised phrase indicates that the person themselves do not know the origin of strength. Additionally it contributes to the depth of the poem, as it offers a limited insight into the person's thoughts. Just a few liners onwards, Senior once again makes use of punctuation to emphasize the person's inner life and add more information to the pictured scene. "To load up with guilt (not a word/ from the ones at the threshold). Not/ a word!" (ll. 5-7). With these words Senior hints at the feelings of guilt caused by their decision to leave. Moreover Senior repeats "[...] not a word [...] Not/ a word!" (l.5-6) to express that while the subject at first tries to suppress the hurt at her family's or friends', who are on the scene when they walk out the door, reaction to her moving out. Also punctuation is used to emphasise their feelings, because Senior first presents the phrase in parentheses before she repeats it with an exclamation mark at the end. This shows the person's frustration in the people's reaction, yet the person walks away.

The traveller's guilt at leaving behind his home and people is depicted in visual terms, since it Senior writes that they "[...] load up with guilt [...]" (l. 5). In reference to Senior's research project *Working Miracles: Women's Lives in the English-speaking Caribbean* explains the especially guilt-laden mother-daughter relationship in literature as well as reality (62-63). If we assume the person to be a female, as Batcos (62) does, then alienating oneself from the home would indicate an alienation from domesticity and its implied values. But even if this were not the case in "Leaving Home", nonetheless departure from home entails a departure from their family's culture. The poet then continues with an accumulation of different kinds of roads, ranging from small, seldomly used roads to large, highly frequented roads; signifying the move from a rural to an urban area:

> You keep walking. Down
> the dirt track, to the lane, to
> the street, to the highways
> of the world. You alone [...] (ll. 7-10)

The quote above furthermore indicates the loneliness of the poem's individual. After leaving behind his home and thus also his family and friends, they experience isolation. This statement is underpinned by its position in the "Islanded" section of *Over the Roofs of the World*. Still the person does not react as the reader of the poem may expect, but instead is described as relieved (ll. 13-14). Their sentiment of freedom is noted in the following lines of "Leaving Home": "You say: I could get used to the lightness" (ll. 13-14). Maybe this person suffered from oppression at home or in their native culture and thus feels freed after leaving it all behind. Batcos offers a similar explanation, as she argues that the individual's freedom stems from her removal from a culture allocating the private sphere to women:

> "No longer encumbered by the obligations in her family, she senses a freedom in her decision, one that Senior equates with the ability to become involved in the *public* sphere rather than remaining tied down to the more self-less demands of domesticity" (Batcos 63)

In spite of describing the migrant as a midwife in the last line of the poem (26), their gender remains vague and therefore Batcos has based her interpretation on ambiguous details, though the profession of a midwife is most often associated with females.

Then the mood of the poem changes with the beginning of the second stanza. Senior no longer portrays the migrant as free, but as bound to their native country or rather isle. After the initial sensation of living away from home passed, the subject begins to feel nostalgia for her home. This change in attitude is brought about, to cite Batcos, "[...] when stretching her freedom to its capacity, 'on a hilltop,' she finally realizes that she [...] lived under the false impression of her liberation" (63). Senior evokes images of the ocean (Batcos 63) with such phrases as "drowning, a movement of ebbing/ and flowing" (ll. 18/19) and by using one central word related to nautical science, 'mooring' (l. 21). Besides, Batcos establishes a connection to the "Islanded" section to which the poem belongs (63). The subject of the poem "[...] failed to detach/ from that mooring" (ll. 20-21), thus they have not been able to cut their connection to their home and are unable to create a new identity in their new place of residence. Comment on the use of parentheses is required again for the reason that Senior creates a contradiction by its use. While the actual line, excluding the parenthetical statement, claim that the individual has noticed its nostalgia early, the parenthesis asserts the opposite (ll. 19-20). A solution to this problematic identity is offered by Senior in the form of the antithesis "Executioner/ Midwife" (ll.25 -26). The executioner on the one hand represents ending a life, while the midwife stands for a new life. In order to create a new identity, Senior professes that you have to choose between your two homes. The connection to one has to be cut by a knife (l. 23) so that the other can come to live. As none of the countries is perfect however, the subject is forced to decide on the one representing the lesser evil so to speak, which is alluded to with "[a]lways, cruelty of choice" (l. 22). This means that they have to resolve their conflicting in-between identity by choosing solely one home, and therefore also identity, and abandon the other. With "Leaving Home" Senior depicts the struggle of a migrant to build a new life and identity, while continuing to be linked to their native country. Surprisingly, the poem conveys the message that you have to terminate all your connections to your homeland to facilitate the creation of a new identity, since the poem ends with the 'midwife' and the metaphor of the midwife represents the new identity.

3 Conclusion

A good deal of progress has been made towards determining how the Caribbean Canadian women writers Claire Harris und Olive Senior deal with the issues of identity in their poetry. Certainly all of the have their induvial approaches, yet they share more similarities than differences in their portrayal of Caribbean Canadian women's identity. Harris and Senior reveal the various components that cause the problematic nature of female diaspora identity. The thesis showed that gender and sexuality affect identity in so far, as they render Caribbean women voiceless in a heteropatriarchal society. Additionally, colonialism rendered their colonial subjects silent by denying them any expression of indigenous cultural identity and rendering the inferior, thus duplicating the pressure on women to be silent. This became clear in the analyses of the influence of the colonial past on cultural as well as individual identity in the poems. It became obvious that that while exploring the history of colonialism in their work of poetry, each poem illuminated a different aspect. Senior illustrated the colonial education system and Brand addressed the importance of language as colonial tool of power. It should not be neglected that both of the writers addressed the problem of racism in Canadian identity in their works, thus challenging the Canadian myth of functional multiculturalism. By facing discrimination at home and in exile, either based their gender or their race, the very existence of a home for black Caribbean Canadian women ultimately called into question.

Although it has been shown that the issue if identity is a central theme in Caribbean literature, it can nonetheless be argued that each author handles the theme in a different way. Due to their own position in cultures of the Caribbean as well as the fact that both women have immigrated to Canada, their work reflects a distinct view on cultural identity. Furthermore Harris and Senior lend voice to the marginalised experience of black Caribbean Canadian women. It is important that they have come to respect women that are rendered voiceless trough both cultures for being the sexual and racial 'Other'. Moreover, analysis of the issues of identity in the Caribbean Canadian poetry by Harris and Senior shows that the traditional concept of identity is increasingly disestablished by globalisation. Instead of conceiving identities to be fixed and stable, societies have to accommodate a growing number of hyphenated identities, people who claim their belonging to several communities. In times of globalisation identities are becoming less a question of identification with either one culture or another, and instead an identification with both, rendering categories of identity more fluid. Due to the development towards multicultural societies, issues of identity will inevitably gain even more significance in various modes of literary production.

4 Works Cited

Batcos, Stephanie. "Lessons from the Writer: Olive Senior's *over the Roofs of the World* and the Interface of the Caribbean-Canadian Reader." *Beyond the Canebrakes : Caribbean Women Writers in Canada.* Ed. Williams, Emily Allen. Trenton, NJ: Africa World Press, 2008. 57-78.

Boi, Paola. "Homecomings without Home: Reconquering the Creole Identity through the Conquest of Discursive Space." *Changing Currents : Transnational Caribbean Literary and Cultural Criticism.* Eds. Williams, Emily Allen and Melvin B. Rahming. Trenton, NJ: Africa World Press, 2006. 167-94.

Boyce Davies, Carol, and Elaine Savory Fido quoted in. "Poetic Negotiation of Identity in the Works of Brathwaite, Harris, Senior, and Dabydeen: Tropical Paradise Lost and Regained." *Caribbean Studies.* Ed. Williams, Emily Allen. Lewiston, NY: Edwin Mellen Press, 1999. 52.

Brown, Stewart, and Mark McWatt. "Introduction." *The Oxford Book of Caribbean Verse.* Eds. Brown, Stewart and Mark McWatt. 2 ed. New York: Oxford University, 2009. XVII-XXXV.

Ede, Amatoritsero. "Exile Is Not My Name." *Sentinel Poetry (Online).*38 (2006). 22. Aug. 2010 <http://www.sentinelpoetry.org.uk/0106/interview.htm>.

Gikandi, Simon. *Writing in Limbo : Modernism and Caribbean Literature.* Ithaca, N.Y.: Cornell University Press, 1992.

Harris, Claire. "Child   This Is the Gospel on Bakes." *The Oxford Book of Caribbean Verse.* Eds. Brown, Stewart and Mark McWatt. 2 ed. New York: Oxford University, 2009. 162-64.

---. *Drawing Down a Daughter.* Fredericton, New Brunswick: Goose Lane Ed., 2007.

---. "Policeman Cleared in Jaywalking Case." *Grammar of Dissent: Poetry and Prose by Claire Harris, M. Nourbese Philip, Dionne Brand.* Ed. Morrell, Carol. Fredericton: Goose Lane Ed., 1994. 48-50.

---. "Why Do I Write." *Grammar of Dissent: Poetry and Prose by Claire Harris, M. Nourbese Philip, Dionne Brand.* Ed. Morrell, Carol. Fredericton: Goose Lane Ed., 1994. 26-33.

Ickstadt, Heinz. "Die Sehnsucht Nach Dem Primitiven Anderen Und Die Harlem Renaissance." *Amerikanische Literaturgeschichte.* Ed. Zapf, Hubert, et. al. 2., aktualisierte Aufl. ed. Stuttgart, Weimar: Metzler, 2004. XII, 589 S. Ill.

Kuwabong, Dannabang. "Reading the Gospel of Bakes: Daughter's Representations of Mothers in the Poetry of Claire Harris and Lorna Goodison." *Canadian Woman Studies/ Les Cahiers De La Femme* 18.2-3 (1998): 132-38 pp. 20 Aug. 2010 <http://pi.library.yorku.ca/ojs/index.php/cws/article/viewFile/8550/7728>.

Lindsay, Vachel. "The Congo: A Study of the Negro Race." *The Congo and Other Poems.* New York: Dover Publications, 1992. 3-7.

Morrell, Carol. *Grammar of Dissent: Poetry and Prose by Claire Harris, M. Nourbese Philip, Dionne Brand.* Fredericton: Goose Lane Ed., 1994.

Papke, Renate. *Poems at the Edge of Difference: Mothering in New English Poetry by Women* 2008. 17 Aug. 2010 <http://webdoc.sub.gwdg.de/univerlag/2008/papke.pdf>.

Pollard, Velma. "An Introduction to the Poetry and Fiction of Olive Senior." *Callaloo* 36 (1988): 540-45.

Rutherford, Anna quoted in. "Poetic Negotiation of Identity in the Works of Brathwaite, Harris, Senior, and Dabydeen: Tropical Paradise Lost and Regained." *Caribbean Studies.* Ed. Williams, Emily Allen. Lewiston, NY: Edwin Mellen Press, 1999. 98.

Senior, Olive. "Birdshooting Season." *Talking of Trees*. Ed. Senior, Olive. Kingston, Jamaica: Calabash, 1985. 2.

---. "Colonial Girls School." *Talking of Trees*. Ed. Senior, Olive. Kingston, Jamaica: Calabash, 1985. 26-27.

---. *Working Miracles: Women's Lives in the English-Speaking Caribbean*. London: James Currey, 1991.

Williams, Emily Allen. "The Ancestral Quilt of Arawak, African, and European Influence in the Poetry of Olive Senior." *Poetic Negotiation of Identity in the Works of Brathwaite, Harris, Senior, and Dabydeen: Tropical Paradise Lost and Regained*. Ed. Williams, Emily Allen. Caribbean Studies. Lewiston, NY: Edwin Mellen Press, 1999. 75-101.

---. "Claire Harris and the Poetic Shape of Women's Words." *Poetic Negotiation of Identity in the Works of Brathwaite, Harris, Senior, and Dabydeen: Tropical Paradise Lost and Regained*. Ed. Williams, Emily Allen. Caribbean Studies. Lewiston, NY: Edwin Mellen Press, 1999. 47-73.

---. *Poetic Negotiation of Identity in the Works of Brathwaite, Harris, Senior, and Dabydeen: Tropical Paradise Lost and Regained*. Caribbean Studies. Lewiston, NY: Edwin Mellen Press, 1999.

---. "Triadric Revelations of Excilic Identity: Claire Harris's *Fables from the Women's Quarters, Dipped in Shadow*, and *She*." *Beyond the Canebrakes : Caribbean Women Writers in Canada*. Ed. Williams, Emily Allen. Trenton, NJ: Africa World Press, 2008. 57-78.

---. "Triadric Revelations of Exilic Identity: Claire Harris's *Fables from the Women's Quarters, Dipped in Shadows*, and *She*." *Beyond the Canebrakes : Caribbean Women Writers in Canada*. Ed. Williams, Emily Allen. Trenton, NJ: Africa World Press, 2008. 57-78.